Published in 2012 by Helen Exley Giftbooks.

12 11 10 9 8 7 6 5 4 3 2

ISBN 978-1-84634-549-4

A copy of the CIP data is available from the British Library.

Printed in China.

Helen Exley Giftbooks,
16 Chalk Hill, Watford, Herts WD19 4BG, UK
www.helenexleygiftbooks.com

A gift of Happiness

ART BY JULIETTE CLARKE

HELEN EXLEY®

Other Helen Exley Giftbooks

Smile

Be What You Believe In

A Special Gift of Peace and Calm

Time to Just Be

Happy Day!

Other books in this series

Be True to Yourself

A Friend...

A gift of Calm

A gift of Hope

The ways of Wisdom

ABOUT THIS BOOK

Einstein once said, "There are two ways to live your life. One is as though nothing is a miracle. The other is as though everything is a miracle." *A Gift of Happiness* contains hundreds of quotations on the wonders of everyday life, of nature, of spring mornings, of the simple joys and happiness to be found in ordinary things. It is a gem of a book, literally "wonder full". Take these thoughts with you. Be happy!

HERE AND NOW

Today a new sun rises for me; everything lives, everything is animated, everything seems to speak to me of my passion, everything invites me to cherish it....

ANNE DE LENCLOS
(1620-1706)

There are two ways to live your life. One is as though nothing is a miracle. The other is as though everything is a miracle.

ALBERT EINSTEIN
(1879-1955)

Love the moment, and the energy of that moment will spread beyond all boundaries.

CORITA KENT
(1918-1986)

Nothing is worth more than this day.

JOHANN
WOLFGANG VON GOETHE
(1749-1832)

Yesterday is a cancelled cheque; tomorrow is a promissory note; today is the only cash you have – so spend it wisely.

KAY LYONS

MAKE HAY WHILE THE SUN SHINES.

PROVERB

That it will never
come again
is what makes life
so sweet.

EMILY DICKINSON (1830-1886)

Enjoy the blessings
of the day...
and the evils bear
patiently; for this day
only is ours:
we are dead to
yesterday, and not born
to tomorrow.

JEREMY TAYLOR
(1613-1667)

I have learned to live each day as it comes, and not to borrow trouble by dreading tomorrow.

DOROTHY DIX
(1802-1887)

LIFE IS IN THE HERE AND NOW, NOT IN THE THERE AND AFTERWARDS.

VIMALA THAKAR,
FROM
"THE ELOQUENCE OF LIVING"

*It is so hard for us
little human beings to accept
this deal that we get.
We get to live, then
we have to die.
What we put into every
moment is all we have....*

GILDA RADNOR,
FROM "IT'S ALWAYS SOMETHING"

One of the most tragic things I know about human nature is that all of us tend to put off living. We are all dreaming of some magical rose garden over the horizon – instead of enjoying the roses that are blooming outside our windows today.

DALE CARNEGIE

It's only when we truly
know and understand
that we have a limited
time on earth –
that we will begin to live
each day to the fullest,
as if it was the only
one we had.

ELISABETH KÜBLER-ROSS,
(1926-2004)

Why not seize
the pleasure at once?
How often
is happiness
destroyed by
preparation,
foolish preparation!

JANE AUSTEN
(1775-1817)

For every person
who has ever lived
there has come, at last,
a spring they will
never see. Glory then
in the springs
that are yours.

PAM BROWN, B.1928

SHARING HAPPINESS, AND FRIENDSHIP

All who joy
would win,
Must share it –
happiness was born
a twin.

LORD BYRON (1788-1824)

Happiness is like a disease. It spreads.

SIMON ELLIOT,
AGE 11

These are the things
I prize and hold
of dearest worth:
Light of
the sapphire skies,
peace of

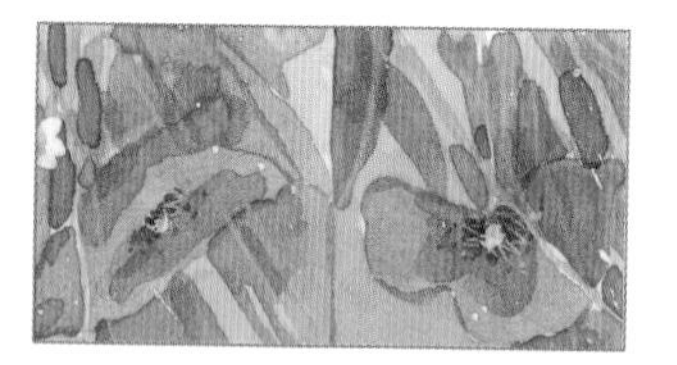

the silent hills,
shelter of forests...
And best of all,
along the way,
friendship and mirth.

HENRY VAN DYKE (1852-1933)

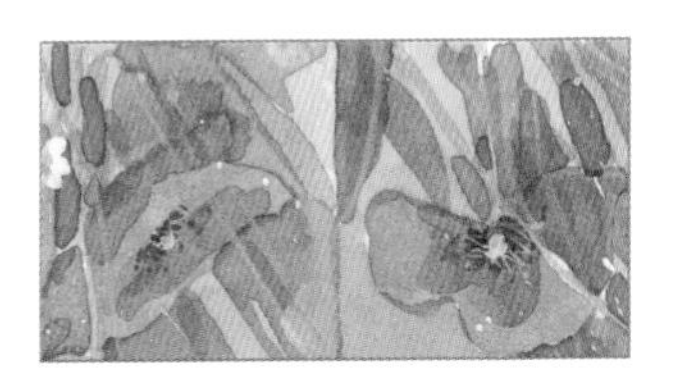

Happiness is in the comfortable companionshi[p] of friends.

PAM BROWN, B.1928

True happiness is of a retired nature, and an enemy to pomp and noise; it arises, in the first place, from the enjoyment of one's self; and, in the next, from the friendship and conversation of a select few companions.

JOSEPH ADDISON (1672-1719)

Happiness is the whole world as friends. It's light all through your life.

DANIEL DILLING,
AGE 8

Here are the veins
of your hand.
Here streams run
to meet the river.
We are bound together.
The same life flows
through all things.
Be happy in this unity,
this continuity.

PAM BROWN, B.1928

Happiness is the feeling which wraps itself around a family.... There is a sense of togetherness which is almost tangible in the warm atmosphere of the room.

SUSIE GREENAWAY, AGE 14

To be able to find joy in another's joy: that is the secret of happiness.

GEORGES BERNANOS
(1888-1948)

I hope you always have room in your life for another friend.

PAM BROWN, B.1928

TRUE JOY IS SERENE

Perfect bliss grows only in the heart made tranquil.

HINDU PROVERB

Still there is joy
that will not cease,
Calm hovering
o'er the face of things,
That sweet tranquillity
and peace
That morning
ever brings.

JOHN CLARE (1793-1864)

Happiness is to seek and find peace of mind.

GILLIAN HUGHES, AGE 11

Close your eyes
and you will
see clearly
Cease to listen
and you will
hear the truth.

TAOIST POEM

Learn to be silent.
Let your quiet mind
listen and absorb.

PYTHAGORAS

Deep in the soul,
below pain, below all
the distraction
of life, is a silence vast
and grand –
an infinite ocean of calm,
which nothing
can disturb. Nature's

own exceeding peace,
which "passes
understanding".
That which we seek...
we find at last
within ourselves.

C.M.C.
QUOTED IN R.M. BUCKE,
"COSMIC CONSCIOUSNESS"

If I could give you anything it would be a quietness at the very heart of your life that would remain tranquil and certain whatever befell.

PAM BROWN, B.1928

You ask why I make my home in the mountain forest, and I smile, and am silent, and even my soul remains quiet: it lives in the other world which no one owns. The peach trees blossom. The water flows.

LI PO (701-762)

The capacity to be alone becomes linked with self-discovery and self-realizatio with becoming aware of one's deepest needs, feelings, and impulses.

ANTHONY STORR

The miracle comes quietl into the mind that stops a instant and is still.

QUOTED IN
"TIME FOR JOY" BY RUTH FISHEL

Contentment is
the philosopher's stone,
which turns all
it toucheth into gold;
the poor man
is rich with it, the rich
man poor without it.

PROVERB

That the birds
of worry and care fly
above your head,
this you cannot change.
But that they build nests
in your hair,
this you can prevent.

CHINESE PROVERB

*There is only one way
to happiness
and that is to cease
worrying about things
which are beyond
the power of our will.*

EPICTETUS
(1ST CENTURY)

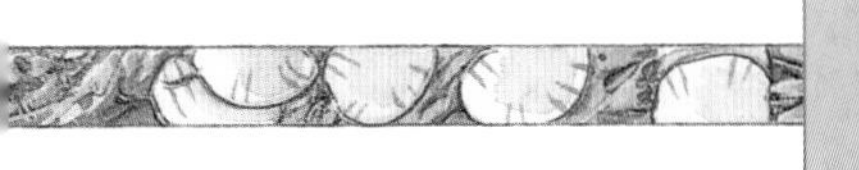

FINDING HAPPINESS IN SMALL EVERYDAY THINGS

Happiness is when everyday things shine like gold.

PAM BROWN, B.1928

Happiness is peace
and freedom,
deep down in our
hearts, the joy of little
childish games,
and jokes and pranks
and laughs. Happiness
is little things,

we treasure in our hearts, to keep them locked and sealed forever....

CLARE SOUTHWELL, AGE 12

Between the house and the store there are little pockets of happiness. A bird, a garden, a friend's greeting... a cat in the sunshine needing a stroke. Recognize them or ignore them. It's always up to you.

PAM BROWN, B.1928

Happiness is thick, oozy mud.

JANE LESLEY GRAY, AGE 12

Happiness is seeing a kitten walking for the first time.

ANDREA WHITE, AGE 10

Be happy
in small things.
They give
great happinesses
the opportunity
to creep up on you,
quietly.

PAM BROWN, B.1928

HAPPINESS IS THE SMELL OF THE AIR ON SUMMER MORNINGS COOL AND CRISP.

LEE WALKER, AGE 8

So you didn't win the Nobel prize but the autumn sun still flickers through the trees and your little cat stretches to touch your face – and someone loves you. And surely that is prize enough?

PAM BROWN, B.1928

Happiness
is lying in bed
on gloomy misty
mornings.

ADRIAN KNIGHT, AGE 10

I wish you the happiness
of a gift from a child;
– a bunch of wilting
dandelions – a fluff-coated
toffee – a frog – a kiss.

PAM BROWN, B.1928

"Henry Rackmeyer, you tel[l]
us what is important."
"A shaft of sunlight
at the end of a dark
afternoon, a note in music
and the way the back
of a baby's neck smells...."
"Correct," said Stuart.
"Those are the
important things."

E.B. WHITE (1899-1985)

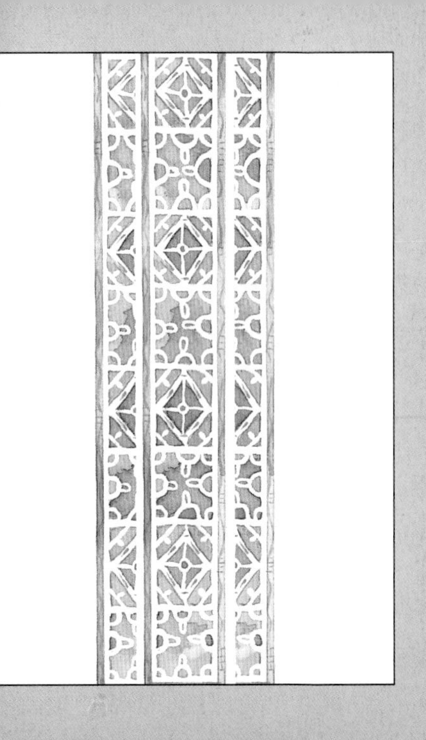

It is the small,
everyday successes
that make
a happy life.

PAM BROWN, B.1928

We act as though comfort and luxury were the chief requirements of life, when all that we need to make us really happy is something to be enthusiastic about.

CHARLES KINGSLEY
(1819-1875)

HAPPINESS IS A QUIET, PERPETUAL REJOICING IN SMALL EVENTS.

PAM BROWN,
B.1928

Happiness is cutting through a fresh, crusty loaf.

CLIVE GARLAND, AGE 12

If you have important work, and enough leisure and income to enable you to do it properly, you are in possession of as much happiness as is good for any of the children of Adam.

R. H. TAWNEY (1880-1962)

To become incredibly
skilful at something,
however small,
an be one of the greatest
happinesses.

PAM BROWN, B.1928

One can only be as happy as happiness. Digging in the garden on a fine spring morning gives as great a happiness as sailing on a millionaire's yacht.

PAM BROWN, B.1928

Is it so small a thing to have enjoyed the sun, to have lived light in the spring, to have loved, to have thought, to have done?

MATTHEW ARNOLD (1822-1888)

HAPPINESS IS WITHIN US

Joy is not
in things; it is
in us.

RICHARD WAGNER
(1813-1883)

I don't think that...
one gets a flash of
happiness once, and
never again;
it is there within you....

ISAK DINESEN (1885-1962)

*Happiness is inward
and not outward; and so it
does not depend on what we
have, but on what we are.*

HENRY VAN DYKE (1852-1933)

Happiness is meant
for everyone
But is elusive as a butterfly.
Happiness is beautiful,
as a flower. It cannot
be expressed in any rhyme.
It may only last a fraction o
an hour. But it stays inside
the heart beyond all time.

E. WRIGHT

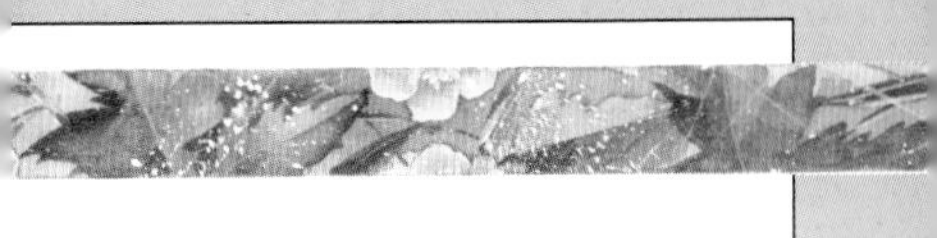

It is not easy
to find happiness
in ourselves,
and it is not
possible to find it
elsewhere.

AGNES REPPLIER
(1858-1950)

The great sea
Has sent me adrift,
It moves me as
the weed in a
great river,
Earth and the
great weather

Move me,
Have carried
me away
And move my
inward parts
with joy.

UVAVNUK

A NEW LIFE BEGINNING FOR YOU

I wish you
the happiness of
letting the past go –
and finding new
beginnings.

PAM BROWN, B.1928

Happiness is essentially a state of going somewhere, wholeheartedly, one directionally, without regret or reservation.

WILLIAM SHELDON

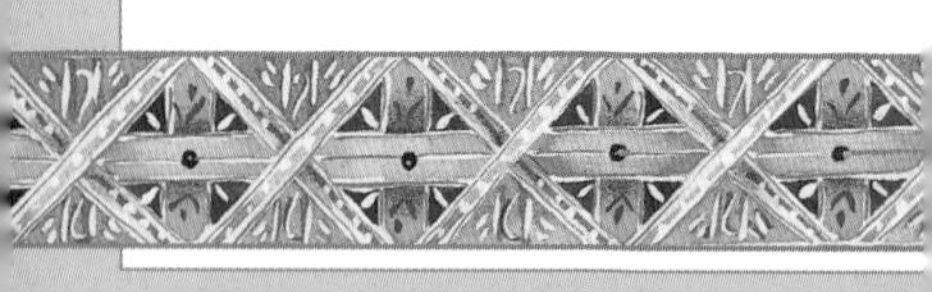

The great successful people of the world... think ahead and create their mental picture, and then go to work, materializing that picture... altering this a bit and that a bit, but steadily building....

ROBERT COLLIER

Thank God every morning when you get up that you have something to do that day which must be done, whether you like it or not.

CHARLES KINGSLEY
(1819-1875)

When you get into
a tight place and
everything goes against yo
till it seems as though yo
could not hold on a minu
longer, never give up ther
for that is just the place
and time that the tide
will turn.

HARRIET BEECHER STOWE
(1811-1896)

A new life begins
for us with every second.
Let us go forward
joyously to meet it....
and we shall walk better
with our eyes before
us than with them
ever cast behind.

JEROME K. JEROME (1859-1927)

Our greatest glory
is not in never falling,
but in rising
every time we fall.

CONFUCIUS (551-479 B.C.)

This is
the astonishment
called Spring.
This is the thaw
when your dull winter
breaks in a rush of joy
– and you are
always young.

PAM BROWN, B.1928

HAPPINESS IN GIVING

In the pursuit of happiness half the world is on the wrong scent. They think it consists in having and getting, and in being served by others. Happiness is really found in giving and in serving others.

HENRY DRUMMOND
(1851-1897)

May no one ever come to you without going away better and happier. Everyone should see kindness in your face, in your eyes, in your smile.

MOTHER TERESA (1910-1997), FROM "HEART OF JOY"

A kind heart
is a fountain of gladness,
making everything
in its vicinity freshen
into smiles.

WASHINGTON IRVING
(1783-1859)

NO JOY CAN EQUAL THE JOY OF SERVING OTHERS.

SAI BABA

Seeking one's own happiness shrinks one's world. Seeking for others' happiness stretches it to unknown horizons.

PAM BROWN, B.1928

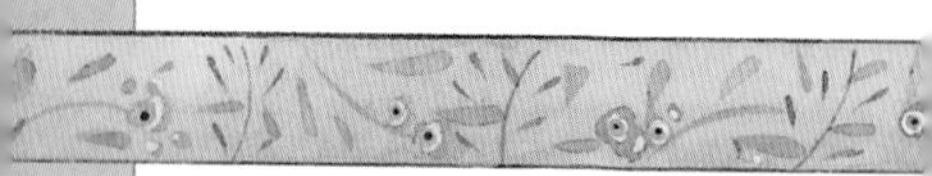

...an act of goodness is in
itself an act of happiness.
It is the flower of a long inner
life of joy and contentment;
it tells of peaceful hours
and days on the sunniest
heights of our soul.

COUNT MAURICE MAETERLINCK
(1862-1949)

One thing I know: the only ones among you who will be really happy are those who will have sought and found how to serve.

ALBERT SCHWEITZER
(1875-1965)

The soul that perpetually overflows with kindness and sympathy will always be cheerful.

PARKE GODWIN

There is a wonderful, mystical law of nature that the three things we crave most in life – happiness, freedom, and peace of mind – are always attained by giving them to someone else.

AUTHOR UNKNOWN

Grief can take care of itself, but to get the full value of a joy, you must have somebody to divide it with.

MARK TWAIN
(1835-1910)

If you have not often felt the joy of doing a kind act, you have neglected much, and most of all yourself.

A. NEILEN

All of us have the power to give happiness... a listening ear, a seeing eye, an outstretched hand.

PAM BROWN, B.1928

TAKING TIME OUT

Never do I close my door behind me without being conscious that I am carrying out an act of charity towards myself.

PETER HØEG

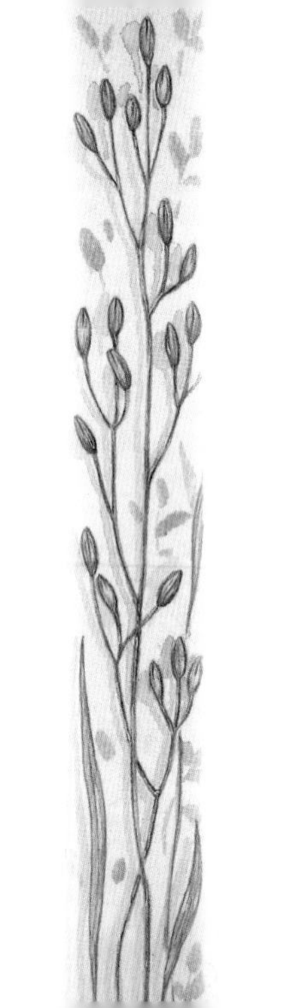

Every form of happiness is private. Our greatest moments are personal, self-motivated, not to be touched. The things which are... precious to us are the things we withdraw from promiscuous sharing.

AYN RAND (1905-1982)

Have the courage
to be alone...
for once try to endure
your own company
for a while....
Don't speak, then, not
even with yourself nor
with the others with

whom we dispute
even when they
are not there. Wait.
Listen....
Endure yourself!

KARL RAHNER (1904-1984)

Learn to take a little time – even if it is a moment in the garden, a gallery, a café. Appreciate it. Let birds and frogs and pictures, music and books and undemanding friends restore you. People need nourishment.

PAM BROWN, B.1928

Solitude is freedom.
It's an anchor, an anchor in
the void. You're anchored
to nothing, and that's my
definition of freedom.

JOHN LILLY

Whenever you're deeply troubled, persuade your mind to concentrate on little, present pleasures. Give yourself time to heal. Be still.

PAM BROWN, B.1928

Whenever I've got time to go somewhere on my bike I feel happy. I am free to go wherever I want. Nobody fussing around me. I'm free as a bird. You can't be happy if you're not free.

KEVIN WILLIAMS, AGE 9

If your nose is close
to the grindstone
And you hold it
there long enough
In time you'll say
there's no such thing
As brooks that
babble and birds

THAT SING
THESE THREE WILL
ALL YOUR
WORLD COMPOSE
JUST YOU, THE STONE
AND YOUR POOR
OLD NOSE.

AUTHOR UNKNOWN,
ON A TWO HUNDRED-YEAR-OLD STONE
IN A COUNTRY CEMETERY

PAIN AND JOY

LIFE IS
A TRAGEDY FULL
OF JOY.

BERNARD MALAMUD

I like living.
I have sometimes been
wildly, despairingly,
acutely miserable,
racked with sorrow,
but through it all
I still know quite
certainly that just to be
alive is a grand thing.

AGATHA CHRISTIE (1890-1976)

I wish I could save you from every sorrow, every disaster, every failure. But then you would be cut off from all other creatures on the planet. It is our heartache as much as our happiness that makes a family or a marriage, or a friendship.

PAM BROWN, B.1928

Accept the pain,
cherish the joys,
resolve the regrets;
then can come the best
of benedictions –
"If I had my life to live
over, I'd do it all
the same."

JOAN MCINTOSH

I wish you the gloom of the garden in winter – and, after months of anticipation, the small, green signs of Spring.

PAM BROWN, B.1928

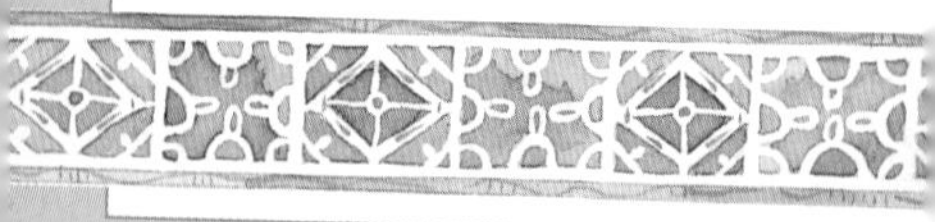

The way I see it,
if you want
the rainbow,
you gotta put up
with the rain.

DOLLY PARTON, B.1946

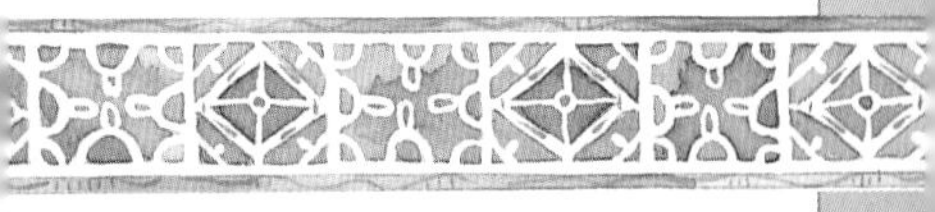

TALK HAPPINESS.
THE WORLD
IS SAD ENOUGH
WITHOUT YOUR
WOE. NO PATH IS
WHOLLY ROUGH.

ELLA WHEELER WILCOX
(1855-1919)

And only when
we are no longer afraid
do we begin to live
in every experience,
painful or joyous;
to live in gratitude for
every moment,
to live abundantly.

DOROTHY THOMPSON
(1894-1961)

LOVE AND KINDNESS

A joyful heart
is the inevitable
result of
a heart burning
with love.

MOTHER TERESA
(1910-1997)

Love and joy are twins, or born of each other.

WILLIAM HAZLITT
(1778-1830)

THOSE WHO BRING SUNSHINE INTO THE LIVES OF OTHERS CANNOT KEEP IT FROM THEMSELVES.

SIR JAMES M. BARRIE
(1860-1937)

The happiness of life
is made up of minute
fractions – the little,
soon-forgotten charities
of a kiss or a smile,
a kind look, or heart-felt
compliment.

SAMUEL TAYLOR COLERIDGE
(1772-1834)

The cure for all
the ills and wrongs,
the cares, the sorrows
and the crimes of
humanity, all lie in
the one word "love."
It is the divine vitality
that everywhere produces
and restores life.

LYDIA M. CHILD (1802-1880)

Happiness is a kind of love. You may think that happiness is just getting things but it isn't really.

SHARON MCNEIL, AGE 11

I am happy.
Because
I am loved.

C. WARMOLL

I wish you the happiness
of love, that does not
change with change,
that shines as surely in age
as in youth.

PAM BROWN, B.1928

It costs nothing to smile at a stranger. It costs nothing to be happy. So go on and spread some around.

JEANETTE ACHILLES, AGE 15

I wish you love. The love of those who lie together in the darkness, talking of times past. The reaching up of children's

arms, the honey-sticky kisses. The reassuring touch, the lighting up of eyes, the sound of a key in the lock.

CHARLOTTE GRAY, B.1937

Happiness
is a perfume
you cannot pour
on others
without getting
a few drops on
yourself.

RALPH WALDO EMERSON
(1803-1882)

The moment you have in your heart this extra-ordinary thing called love and feel the depth, the delight, the ecstasy of it, you will discover that for you the world is transformed.

J. KRISHNAMURTI (1895-1986)

I expect to pass through life but once. If therefore, there be any kindness I can show, or any good thing I can

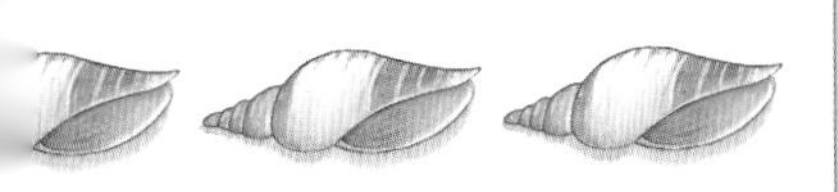

do to any fellow
being, let me
do it now, and not
defer or neglect it,
as I shall not pass
this way again.

WILLIAM PENN

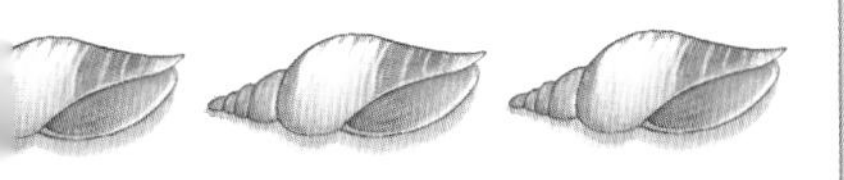

SURPRISED BY JOY!

The moments of happiness we enjoy take us by surprise. It is not that we seize them, but that they seize us.

ASHLEY MONTAGU
(1905-1999)

HAPPINESS SNEAKS
IN THROUGH A DOOR
YOU DIDN'T KNOW YOU
LEFT OPEN.

JOHN BARRYMORE
(1882-1942)

There is no such thing
as the pursuit of happiness,
but there is the discovery
of joy.

JOYCE GRENFELL (1910-1979)

We are surrounded
by happiness.
We trip over it.
The trouble is,
we keep scanning
the horizon
for its coming.

PAM BROWN, B.1928

Happiness is as a butterfly, which, when pursued, is always beyond our grasp, but which, if you will sit down quietly, may alight upon you.

NATHANIEL HAWTHORNE
(1804-1864)

One must
never look
for happiness:
one meets
it by
the way....

ISABELLE EBERHARDT
(1877-1904)

So long as man is alive
and free, he will, in one
way or another, seek that
which gives him pleasure.
But to seek is not
necessarily to find....
The basis of happiness is
abundance of life,
and abundance of life
is a real thing....

DAVID STARR JORDAN
(1851-1931)

He who bends
to himself a joy
Doth the wingèd
life destroy;
But he who kisses
a joy as it flies
Lives in Eternity's
sunrise.

WILLIAM BLAKE
(1757-1827)

*When one door
of happiness closes,
another opens;
but often we look so long
at the closed door
that we do not see
the one which
has been opened for us.*

HELEN KELLER
(1880-1968)

Many run about
after happiness
like an absent-minded
man hunting
for his hat, while
it is in his hand or
on his head.

JAMES SHARP (1613-1679)

You were made
for enjoyment, and
the world was filled
with things which
you will enjoy,
unless you are too
proud to be pleased
with them,
or too grasping

to care for what
you can
not turn to other
account than
mere delight.

JOHN RUSKIN (1819-1900)

They seemed
to come suddenly
upon happiness
as if they had
surprised a
butterfly in the
winter woods....

EDITH WHARTON
(c.1862-1937)

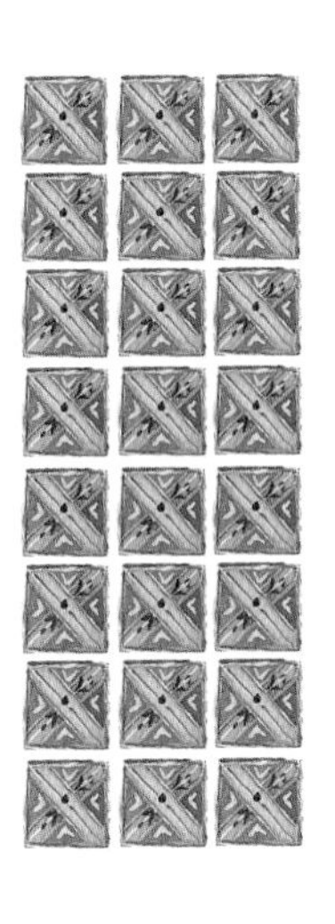

The pursuit of
happiness is a most
ridiculous phrase:
if you pursue
happiness
you'll never find it.

C. P. SNOW (1905-1980)

The happiness of life
is so nice a thing that,
like the sensitive
plant, it shrinks away,
even upon
thinking of it.

JOSEPH SPENCE (1699-1768)

My life has no purpose
no direction, no aim,
no meaning, and yet
I'm happy. I can't figure
it out. What am
I doing right?

CHARLES M. SCHULZ
(1922-2000)

BEAUTY IS ALL ABOUT YOU

Happiness is a lot of things; it's snow, it's sun, it's a thing which every day brings. Happiness is all the world, the beautiful things around.

EMMA SMITH, AGE 7

My heart leaps up when I behold A rainbow in the sky: So was it when my life began; So is it now I am a man: So be it when I shall grow old, Or let me die!

WILLIAM WORDSWORTH
(1770-1850)

*One does not need to...
meditate for hours at a time
to experience the sense of
sublime mystery which
constantly envelops us.
All one need do is notice
intelligently, if even
for a brief moment,
a blossoming tree, a forest
flooded with autumn colors,
an infant smiling.*

SIMON GREENBERG

Earth's crammed with heaven.

ELIZABETH
BARRETT BROWNING
(1806-1861)

Above the roar of city squares the starlings swirl like smoke. In concrete canyons the kestrels raise their young. The wasteland is ablaze with willow-herb. Beauty is all about you.

PAM BROWN, B.1928

Happiness is
the sun in the sky,
galloping on
the beach,
water splashing,
feeling free.

MEGHAN SIMMONS,
AGE 11

You will never
enjoy the world
aright till the sea
itself floweth in
your veins,
till you are clothed
with the heavens
and crowned with
the stars.

THOMAS TRAHERNE

For new, and new, and ever new,
The golden bud within the blue;
And every morning seems to say:
"There's something happy
on the way...."

HENRY VAN DYKE (1852-1933)

...the little hills rejoice on every
side. The pastures are clothed
with flocks; the valleys also
are covered over with corn;
they shout
for joy, they also sing.

PSALMS 65: 12-13

I cannot believe
that the inscrutable
universe turns on
an axis of suffering;
surely the strange
beauty of the world
must somewhere rest
on pure joy!

LOUISE BOGAN
(1897-1970)

HAPPINESS IS A FOREST WITH SCARCELY A SOUND BUT BLUEBELLS GROWING EVERYWHERE.

GAYNOR CHALLINGSWORTH,
AGE 10

Happiness is kicking up the dry Autumn leaves in Saltram Woods.

STUART LANCEY, AGE 7

The sun does not shine for a few trees and flowers, but for the wide world's joy.

HENRY WARD BEECHER
(1813-1877)

I am happy
because the birds
sing to me.

JOSEPHINE, AGE 6

My soul's reverence
for creation increases
every time I behold
the miracle
of a sunset or
the beauty of
the moon.

MAHATMA GANDHI
(1869-1948)

Happiness is
the breaking of
a summer morning.

KIM MILLER, AGE 10

*I wish you the delight
of plants – the small
miracles of graft and
cutting, seed and bulb
and corm. Of new life
from the earth.*

PAM BROWN, B.1928

THE HAPPY ONES SEE ONLY BEAUTIFUL THINGS.

JEREMY LATIMER,
AGE 10

Long after I have forgotten all my human loves, I shall still remember the smell of a gooseberry leaf, or the feel of wet grass on my bare feet. In the long run, it is this feeling that makes life worth living....

GWEN RAVERAT

THE SECRETS OF HAPPINESS

When you finally allow yourself to trust joy and embrace it, you will find you dance with everything.

EMMANUEL

THERE ARE SO MANY WAYS OF BEING HAPPY THAT IT IS FUNNY HOW SOME PEOPLE HAVE TO BE UNHAPPY.

WENDY MCKERNAN, AGE 12

LEARN TO VALUE YOURSELF, WHICH MEANS TO FIGHT FOR YOUR HAPPINESS.

AYN RAND (1905-1982)

There is no duty we so much underrate as the duty of being happy.

ROBERT LOUIS STEVENSON (1850-1894)

If it be my lot to crawl,
I will crawl contentedly:
if to fly, I will fly
with alacrity;
but as long as I can
possibly avoid it,
I will never be unhappy.

SYDNEY SMITH
(1771-1845)

One is happy as a result of one's own efforts, once one knows the necessary ingredients of happiness – simple tastes, a certain degree of courage, self-denial to a point, love of work, and above all, a clear conscience. Happiness is no vague dream, of that I now feel certain.

GEORGE SAND
(AMANDINE AURORE LUCIE DUPIN)
(1804-1876)

Far away there in the sunshine are my highest aspirations. I may not reach them, but I can look up and see their beauty, believe in them, and try to follow where they lead.

LOUISA MAY ALCOTT
(1832-1888)

SMILES, LAUGHTER & MIRTH

Happiness is
my family laughing
People laughing
Mummy kissing
us good night.
It's all lovely.

EMMA POLAND, AGE 8

I wish you laughter.
Spluttering laughter, whooping laughter, the helpless silent laughter that sends you to the floor in tears.
Giggling laughter, heads together....Kind laughter, laughter that reaches out and gathers others to itself. And never mind who stares.

PAM BROWN, B.1928

A Child of Happiness always seems like an old soul iving in a new body, and her face is very serious until she miles, and then the sun lights up the world....

ANNE CAMERON, B.1938

A happy couple share a certain smile that no one else quite understands.

PAM BROWN, B.1928

*The most wasted day
of all is that
on which we have
not laughed.*

SEBASTIEN
R. N. CHAMFORT
(1741-1794)

THE ONE WHO SMILES RATHER THAN RAGES IS ALWAYS THE STRONGER.

JAPANESE WISDOM

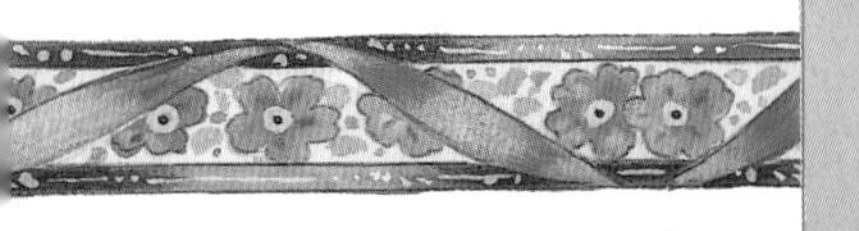

Some people have a beautiful smile and when people see it they feel happy.

SUSANNAH MORRIS, AGE 10

A beaming smile
is just that –
it lights up
the room like
a beacon.

PAM BROWN, B.1928

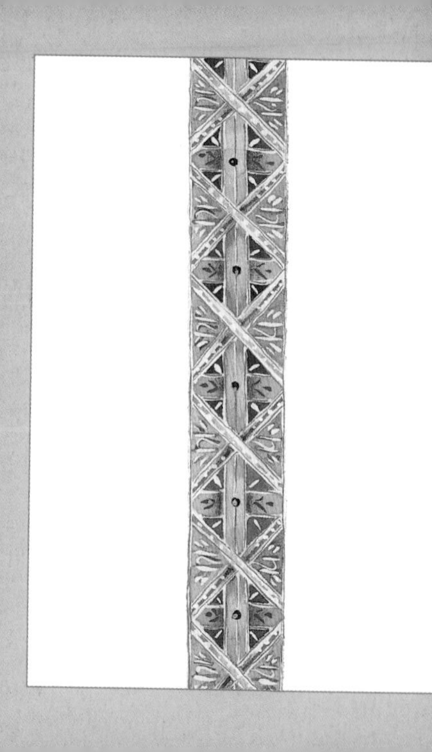

O wonderful,
wonderful, and
most wonderful
wonderful, and yet
again wonderful,
and after
that out of all
whooping!

WILLIAM SHAKESPEARE
(1564-1616),
FROM "AS YOU LIKE IT"

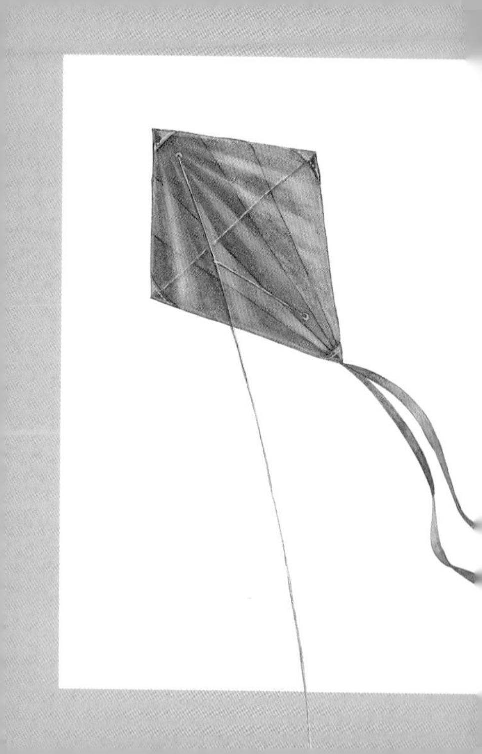

When I feel so
happy, I jump
to touch the sky,
When I feel so
happy, I climb
a mountainside.
When I feel so
happy, I run around
the world.

ANDREW MOSS, AGE 10

I don't know where our humor comes from, but it can be the worst situation in the whole world a nd you can sit there and you can laugh. I guess it's just because the good inside of us always comes out no matter when or where it is.

RENNE HALLETT
(TONAWANDA SENECA)

Frame your mind
to mirth and merriment,
which bars a thousand
harms and
lengthens life.

WILLIAM SHAKESPEARE
(1564-1616)

To a young heart
everything is fun.

CHARLES DICKENS
(1812-1870)

Take time to laugh
– It is the music
of the soul.

OLD ENGLISH PRAYER

If you're not allowed to laugh in heaven, I don't want to go there.

MARTIN LUTHER
(1483-1546)

LIVING LIFE TO THE FULL

Write it on your heart that every day is the best day in the year.

RALPH WALDO EMERSON
(1803-1882)

Life is fun
Life is happiness
Life is gladness
Life is loving
Life is helping
Life is gentleness
Life is laughter
Oh, life is beautiful

ALLISON HUDDART, AGE 10

I will not die an unlived life. I will not live in fear of falling or catching fire.

DAWNA MARKOVA

Existence is a strange bargain.
Life owes us little;
we owe it everything.
The only true happiness comes
from squandering ourselves
for a purpose.

WILLIAM COWPER
(1731-1800)

To fill the hour – that is happiness; to fill the hour, and leave no crevice for a repentance or an approval.

RALPH WALDO EMERSON
(1803-1882)

They are committing murder who merely live.

MAY SARTON (1912-1995),
FROM SUMMARY IN
"INNER LANDSCAPE"

Every year I live
I am more convinced that
the waste of life lies in
the love we have not given,
the powers we have not
used, the selfish
prudence that will
risk nothing...

MARY CHOLMONDELEY

Life was meant
to be lived and
curiosity must be
kept alive. One must
never, for whatever
reason, turn one's
back on life.

ELEANOR ROOSEVELT
(1884-1962)

Believe that life is worth living and your belief will help create that fact.

WILLIAM JAMES
(1842-1910)

People for the sake of getting a living forget to live.

MARGARET FULLER
(1810-1830),
FROM "SUMMER
ON THE LAKES"

I'd been busy, busy,
so busy, preparing
for life, while life
floated by me, quiet
and swift
as a regatta.

LORENE CARY,
FROM "BLACK ICE"

People do not
live nowadays –
they get about
ten percent
out of life.

ISADORA DUNCAN
(1878-1927)

I WAS MERELY
A DISINTERESTED
SPECTATOR AT
THE BANQUET
OF LIFE.

ELAINE DUNDY,
FROM "THE DUD
AVOCADO"

I wish you the happiness of ideas, the excitement of reason, the triumph of understanding, the clearing of sight, the sharpening of

hearing, the reaching
out to new
discovery, a pleasure
in the past as well
as in the present.
I wish you the joy
of creativity.

PAM BROWN, B.1928

Life engenders life.
Energy creates energy.
It is by spending oneself
that one becomes rich.

SARAH BERNHARDT
(1844-1923), IN
"MADAME SARAH"

*The sense of existence
is the greatest happiness.*

BENJAMIN DISRAELI
(1804-1881)

I have felt to soar
in freedom
and in the fullness
of power,
joy, volition.

WALT WHITMAN
(1819-1892)

If you want
to be happy, be.

LEO TOLSTOY
(1828-1910)

Do not linger
to gather flowers
to keep them,
but walk on,
for flowers will keep
themselves
blooming all
your way.

RABINDRANATH TAGORE
(1861-1941)

WHAT IS A HELEN EXLEY GIFTBOOK

Helen Exley Giftbooks cover the most powerful of all human relationships: the bonds within families and between friends, and the theme of personal values. No expense is spared in making sure that each book is as meaningful a gift as it is possible to create: good to give, good to receive. You have the result in your hands. If you have loved it – tell others! There is no power on earth like the word-of-mouth recommendation of friends!

Helen Exley Giftbooks
16 Chalk Hill,
Watford, Herts
WD19 4BG, UK

www.helenexleygiftbooks.com

All words from Helen Exley's collection
of happiness quotations.

Acknowledgements:
The publishers are grateful for permission to reproduce copyright material.
Whilst every reasonable effort has been made to trace copyright holders,
the publishers would be pleased to hear from any not here acknowledged.